# Amphibian Babies

Catherine Veitch

Raintree

Raintree is an imprint of Capstone Global Library Limited, a company incorporated in England and Wales having its registered office at 7 Pilgrim Street, London, EC4V 6LB – Registered company number: 6695582

www.raintreepublishers.co.uk
myorders@raintreepublishers.co.uk

Text © Capstone Global Library Limited 2013
First published in hardback in 2013
Paperback edition first published in 2014
The moral rights of the proprietor have been asserted.

Edited by Daniel Nunn, Rebecca Rissman, and Catherine Veitch
Designed by Cynthia Della-Rovere
Picture research by Ruth Blair
Production by Victoria Fitzgerald
Originated by Capstone Global Library
Printed and bound in China

ISBN 978 1 406 25922 3 (hardback)
17  16  15  14  13
10 9 8 7 6 5 4 3 2 1

ISBN 978 1 406 25929 2 (paperback)
18  17  16  15  14
10 9 8 7 6 5 4 3 2 1

**British Library Cataloguing in Publication Data**
Veitch, Catherine.
Amphibian babies. -- (Animal babies)
597.8'1392-dc23
A full catalogue record for this book is available from the British Library.

**Acknowledgements**
We would like to thank the following for permission to reproduce photographs: iStockphoto p. 12 (© Robert Ellis);Naturepl pp. title page (© Nature Production), 6 (© Todd Pusser), 7 (© Visuals Unlimited), 8 (© Doug Wechsler), 10 (© Nature Production), 13 (© Fabio Liverani), 14 (© Bernard Castelein), 16 (© Edwin Giesbers), 17 (© Philippe Clement), 20 (© Inaki Relanzon), 21 (© Rod Williams), 23 (© Doug Wechsler); Shutterstock pp. 4 (© ihsan Gercelman, © Matteo photos), 5 (© Tom C Amon, © Bo Valentino, © Melinda Fawve, © Ryan M. Bolton), 9 (© Ian Grainger), 11 (© Dirk Ercken), 15, 18 (© ethylalkohol), 19 (© Cathy Keifer), 22 (© Eric Isselée, © DJTaylor), 23 (© Ian Grainger, © Dirk Ercken).

Front cover photograph of a Japanese tree frog reproduced with kind permission of Naturepl (© Nature Production).

We would like to thank Michael Bright for his invaluable help in the preparation of this book.

Every effort has been made to contact copyright holders of material reproduced in this book. Any omissions will be rectified in subsequent printings if notice is given to the publisher.

# Contents

# What is an amphibian?

Amphibians live on land.
Amphibians also live in water.

frog

toad

newt

salamander

Frogs and toads are amphibians.
Newts and salamanders are
amphibians.

5

# How are most baby amphibians born?

eggs

Most amphibians lay their eggs in water.

Some amphibians lay their eggs
on land.

spawn

Most amphibians lay their eggs in a jelly. This is called spawn.

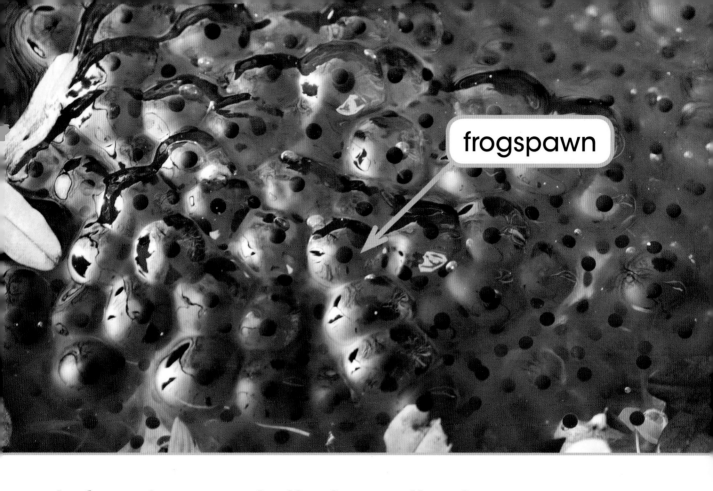

frogspawn

A frog's egg jelly is called
frogspawn.

larva

A larva hatches from each egg.

larva

parent

The larva does not look like
its parent.

# Growing up

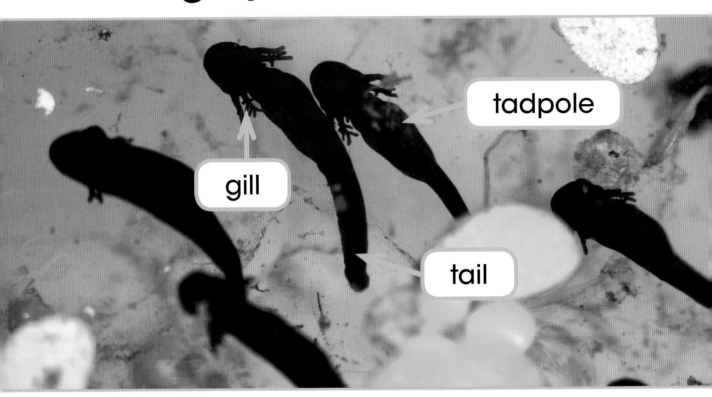

tadpole

gill

tail

Frog larvae are called tadpoles.
Tadpoles have tails and gills.

The tadpoles grow legs.

The tadpoles lose their tails and gills. The tadpoles grow into froglets.

The froglets grow into frogs. The
frogs are ready to leave the water.

# Live amphibian babies

Some amphibians give birth to live babies.

adult

baby

Many of these amphibian babies look like the adults.

# Caring for babies

Most baby amphibians look after themselves. They find a new home.

They catch their own food.

eggs

Some amphibians care for their eggs.

Some amphibians care for
their larvae.

# Life cycle of an amphibian

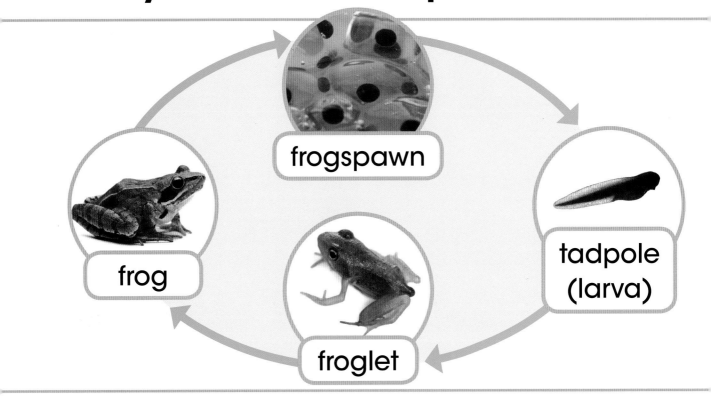

frogspawn

tadpole (larva)

froglet

frog

A life cycle shows the different stages of an animal's life. This is the life cycle of a frog.

22

# Picture glossary

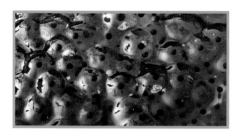 **frogspawn** frogs' eggs in a jelly

 **larva** stage some amphibians have when they first hatch. More than one is larvae.

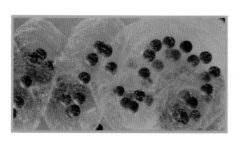 **spawn** eggs of some animals such as frogs that are in a jelly

# Index

**Notes for parents and teachers**

**Before reading**

Show children a collection of photos and videos of amphibians. National Geographic and BBC Nature are useful websites. Explain what an amphibian is and discuss the characteristics of amphibians.

**After reading**

- Mount photos of adult and baby amphibians on card, and play games of snap and pairs where the children have to match a baby amphibian with its parent. Model the correct pairs first.

- Ask children to label the parts of an amphibian: for example, head, feet, tail, scales.

- Look at page 22 and discuss the life cycle stages of an amphibian. Mount photos of the eggs, larvae, baby, and adult stages and ask children to put the photos in order. Encourage children to draw a life cycle of a human to compare. Compare how different amphibians care for their babies. Discuss the care human babies need.

- To extend children's knowledge, the amphibians are as follows: frogs: p4; salamander eggs: p6; salamander: p7; toad eggs: p8; frogspawn: p9; salamander larva: p10; crested newt: p11; frog tadpole: pp12, 13; frog: pp14, 15; lizard: p16; salamander: p17; frog: pp18, 19; toad: p20; poison arrow frog: p21.